MW00975234

Amazing Healing Encounters

Real Life Miracles
and the Lessons they Taught Me

Andy Hayner

Copyright © 2016 Andy Hayner

All rights reserved. This book is protected by the copyright laws of the United States of America. This book may not be copied or reprinted for commercial gain or profit. The use of short quotations or occasional page copying for personal or group study is permitted and encouraged. Scripture quotations are from the ESV® Bible (The Holy Bible, English Standard Version®), copyright © 2001 by Crossway, a publishing ministry of Good News Publishers. Used by permission. All rights reserved.

ISBN: 1530500184

ISBN-13: 978-1530500185

DEDICATION

To Noel Dawn, my oldest daughter.

May you always shine with the light of Christ
Even in dark places at the darkest of times.
May many rejoice to see His light
As your voice rings out with His praise.

I love you.

*"The people dwelling in darkness have seen a great light,
and for those dwelling in the region and shadow of death,
on them a light has dawned."* (Matt. 4:16)

CONTENTS

ACKNOWLEDGMENTS

This book could never be written without the love and support of my beautiful wife, Tina and the support of my children. You are amazing!

I'd also like to thank my "Full Speed" ministry partners. Your generosity, prayers, and encouragement make it possible for me to devote myself full-time to mobilizing believers to walk in the fullness of Jesus Christ worldwide. Thank you for running with us into the battle! You share in every one of my victories.

Lastly, I'd like to thank Curry Blake and the good people of John G. Lake Ministries. I stand stronger because you've allowed me to stand together with you. Curry, your devotion to the Word of God and amazing teaching has opened my eyes to see God more clearly than I ever would have seen on my own. I'm sure you'll see your finger prints on many of the things I teach. I thank God for you.

PREFACE

Until about fifteen years ago, I was influenced to believe that the miracles of the New Testament were something to read about, not something to expect today. Then God opened my eyes to the simple truth that the Christian life was far more than applying Biblical principles to my own life. It was Jesus Christ Himself who lives in me actually living His life through me.

The lifestyle of Jesus hasn't changed. It's filled with grace, power, truth, and love. It's His life that changes ours. As we learn to cooperate with the presence of His Spirit, He can truly continue to do the works we read about in the gospels through us today, just as He said.

"Truly, truly, I say to you, whoever believes in me will also do the works that I do; and greater works than these will he do, because I am going to the Father." (John 14:12)

In this book you will read about miracles that I have experienced personally in my ministry. Yes, they all really happened. In fact, these stories are but the tip of the iceberg. Yet these are the encounters that I find myself sharing with others as I go about mobilizing believers to walk in the fullness of Jesus Christ. They are hand-picked, not only to share the testimony of God's goodness to inspire your faith. They also pack powerful lessons that will help you walk out the truth of who you are in Christ. I share them with you in the hopes of encouraging you let Jesus Christ freely operate through you in all His fullness to set the captives free wherever you go.

CHAPTER 1
I FEEL LIKE I GOT MY LIFE BACK

When I was in very early stages of learning to walk in the fullness of Jesus, I was taking time to hang out at a local college campus to look for opportunities to advance the Kingdom. I had still not learned how to approach people with love and boldness very well, so I had adopted an approach of sitting on the end of a bench in a crowded area of the student union. I found that if I put my book bag on the ground and dug around in it, people would feel like the remainder of the bench was unoccupied and come and sit next to me. It sounds funny to me now, but that's how I got started.

One afternoon, as I was posted on my corner of the bench, a young man in a black trench coat came to sit on the other end of the bench. I perked up and tried to start a conversation, "How's it going today?" He reluctantly grunted, "Fine." I asked a few more questions and made a few more comments, each of which went nowhere. This guy obviously wanted to keep to himself and was doing everything he could to send me signals to discourage me from talking with him any further.

Finally, when I could think of no more subtle ways to try to engage him in friendship, I just blurted out, "You must need a miracle. What is it?" He sat up straight, his mouth dropped open, and stared at me wide-eyed. I repeated the question with the explanation, "You see, I'm not even a student here. I come up here on my lunch break to pray for people. Whenever I come, I always tell God to put me near people who need miracles. You could have sat anywhere on this campus, but you came and sat right next to me on my bench. So you must need a miracle. What is it?"

At this point, he finally showed some signs of life. "I'm not even sure there is a god. How can you be sure?"

I responded, "I realize that not everyone believes or is sure. That's why I didn't ask you about what you *believed*. I asked you about what you *needed*. IF God is real (and I believe that He is) what miracle do you need in your life?"

He said, "IF God is real, I'm mad at him."

Wanting to understand more, I enquired, "Why are you mad at God? What did God do to you?" I asked this, not because I believe that we should ever presume to judge God or that God had done anything wrong. I just wanted to understand more about where this young man was coming from. God doesn't need us to rush to His defense with arguments. God wants us to reconcile people to God by representing Him, which is far different.

This young man then began to open up, "I've been in constant pain since I've been twelve years old. There was a time when I prayed a lot to be healed, but He didn't do anything. So I gave up and decided that God either isn't real or doesn't care."

I said, "I believe God heard your prayer. I believe that God's about to show you how real He is and how much He cares. Where is your pain?"

He said, "I hurt all over."

"Does it hurt anywhere specific?" I asked.

"It moves around," he said.

"Does it hurt anywhere specific *right now?*" I persisted.

He finally gave me what I was looking for, "It always hurts in my legs."

At this point I said, "Well I'm going to pray for you so that you can be healed right now. I'm going to put my hand on your leg and pray."

At this he shrugged, rolled his eyes, and said, "Knock yourself out," with a "whatever makes you happy" kind of look on his face.

As I moved off the bench to kneel in front of him, I began to stretch my hands towards his knees. Then he raised his voice to almost a shout and said, "Ouch! That hurts!" I hadn't even touched him yet! Immediately, I recognized that whatever demons were afflicting him were digging in hard as they saw me beginning to lay hands on him. So I quickly put my hands just above his knees and firmly said, "Everything causing him pain, GO! Go now! In Jesus' Name!"

The young man instantly relaxed and sat back with a sigh. Instructed him, "Move your legs now." He did and looked confused. I said to him, "Why don't you stand up and move around." He stood up and began moving. As he moved, he was looking around on the ground around his feet, like he dropped his keys or something. He had lost his pain and was wondering what happened to it!

I said, "It's gone isn't it?" At this point, the young man reached into his pocket and pulled out a orange bottle of prescription pills, which I assumed to be pain killers. He said, "It could just be these."

"You were in pain before I prayed. Then I prayed and your pain is all gone. Did you pop those in your mouth while I was praying?" I said with a smile.

Now he was really confused. I could tell his mind was reeling, searching for an answer as to what he was experiencing. I suggested that we walk together for a little bit to make sure his pain was all gone. As we walked I spoke with him, "I know this probably seems to good to be true. But God is real and He loves you! You seem a little confused, so as we walk, let me give you a little bit of perspective. You see, this pain that's been crippling your life wasn't from God. Jesus said, "The thief comes to steal, kill, and destroy but I've come that they may have life in abundance." This pain that came into your life was stealing your health, destroying your life, and trying to kill you. That was from the devil, not from God. God heals people and gives them life. He doesn't make people sick."

I continued, "The devil is a thief who loves to take the good things that God gives us. He's also a liar and an accuser. Here's what I believe probably happened. When you first got sick, you started thinking, "What have I done to deserve this?" The devil was accusing you, as if you were the one to blame for this sickness. You probably confessed every sin you could think of, but nothing changed. Then, the devil started accusing God and bringing thoughts like, "God's not real. If He is, He doesn't care." The devil is a liar. God is real. God does care. He loves you so much He became a man in Jesus Christ. He lived a life of perfect love for you. He healed the sick and took on hell for you. He died for your sins, and rose again to break the power of guilt and death for you. And He just healed you to show you that He's not against you. He's for you. Everything He ever did, He did for you. What He did for your body, He can do for your whole life!"

At this point, the young man was fighting back tears. As we walked, he mostly just listened. I could tell that he was needing some more time to process what was going on. I felt like I had said enough. It was time to give him some space to allow the Holy Spirit to work in his life.

As we parted ways I said, "I'm really glad we met. I'm excited about what God's done for you. I'm going to give you my card with my phone number on it. Understand, I'm not recruiting for anything. I don't need you to come to my church. I've got plenty of stuff to do. But if you'd ever like to call and talk or to grab a soda together, let me know."

With that, we parted ways.

I really wasn't expecting him to call me. People hardly ever call. Jesus healed ten lepers and only one "called back". Kingdom ministry is a lifestyle, not a quick fix church growth gimmick. It's giving freely what we've freely received. More than calling me back, I'm usually hoping that people can check out the free teaching videos on the website I have listed on my card.

In this instance, I got a call late the same evening. I picked up the phone and heard my new friend's voice, "Hello. Do you remember me? We met today at the campus." "Yes, I remember you. How are you doing?" I replied.

"Dude! You fixed it!" He said.

I chuckled, "That was Jesus! He's the one who healed you. He loves you man."

He said, "I know. I know. But you don't understand. I've had medically induced lupus for years and now I don't have it anymore. I've been waiting for the other shoe to drop all day. I haven't taken any pain killers all day, and I don't have any pain, and I've not had any withdrawals from my pain meds either. I'm completely fine."

I said, "That's great! I'm so happy for you. What Jesus did in your body, He wants to do for your whole life." I went on to discuss with him about returning to God and starting to grow in his relationship with God.

As we closed the conversation, he said, "I haven't felt this good for as long as I can remember. I've been so miserable. I've either been too stoned on pain killers to do anything or, if I stop taking my pain meds, I've been in too much pain. But I feel fine and I haven't taken any pain killers all day." Then he said this, "I feel like I got my life back."

That's just what Jesus said, "The thief comes to steal, kill, and destroy, but I've come that they would have life abundantly." (John 10:10)

Living Lessons:
- **God can heal people through your faith, even when they don't have any faith for themselves.**
  This young man was mad at God, skeptical, and just barely willing to allow me to pray, yet God healed Him. He had no faith, but Jesus said that "*believers will lay hands on the sick, and they will recover.*" (Mark 16:18). We can be the believers for others, even when they have serious doubts.

- **The enemy speaks to people through his attacks on their body.** The devil used this attack of lupus to drive a wedge between this person and God. This is a common strategy of the enemy to turn people's hearts against God.

- **God speaks to people through healing.** God used this healing, coupled with the message of the gospel, to restore this person's faith in Jesus Christ.

- **You can love people whether they like you or not.** My goal was not to make this person like me. I wanted to show him the love of God. God can give us the grace to go around "just leave me alone" attitudes and break through with His love.

- Many people are "mad at God" because they've interpreted God through painful circumstances and have attributed attacks from the evil one to God.

CHAPTER 2
IT'S ALWAYS ALL JESUS

I love being close to God. But there are times that I don't "feel" particularly close. I'm not someone who goes through life looking for emotional goosebumps. I just know that there are times when I'm aware that my own heart isn't in a particularly great state. At the moment, I'm just more occupied with things like getting a cup of coffee than with enjoying the love of God or with loving others.

This was one of those mornings.

I was awakened a little after 5:00 a.m. by my youngest daughter. She wouldn't let me escape under the covers. "Get up Daddy! You promised to take me fishing! Get up. Get up." I had promised, but this early?!?!

After gathering our gear, and loading it into the car, I remembered that I would need to get a fishing license. It was so early in the morning that, I recall wondering if Walmart would even be open yet when we arrived. It was open. We entered and walked to the sporting good section to find there was no one at the counter to help us. As we waited for someone to come to the counter so we could purchase a fishing license, I wasn't feeling really spiritual. In fact, I was feeling tired and a little grumpy. I remember thinking, "With all the things that Walmart sells, why can't you get a cup of coffee here?"

Just as I had this thought, a man walked behind us pushing his shopping cart. I couldn't help but notice a pair of crutches laid crossways in the cart. As the man walked by, he had one shoe on with his other foot and ankle heavily wrapped in an ace bandage. He was also walking with a pronounced limp.

I knew that this was on obvious opportunity for me to show this man the love of God by healing his ankle. I hesitated for just a moment because I wasn't feeling very spiritually prepared. However, I knew that lingering in this hesitation was only going to cause me to pass up this opportunity all together. I said, "Okay Jesus. This is all you," and began to walk over to the man with a smile. Even as I stepped, I could hear the Lord chuckle His reply, "It's ALWAYS *all Me.*" I agreed with a smile.

"What happened to your foot," I said to the man. He told me his story. "Can you believe this? I'm actually supposed to be running a marathon today, but I spent four hours in the emergency room over this last night." Again, I asked, "So what happened?" He continued, "I'm a delivery driver and I was finishing up my day, ready for the weekend. I wasn't paying attention like I should've been. I had a big box in my arms and thought I was stepping down onto a platform on my truck. I missed the platform and dropped eighteen inches and rolled my ankle."

I said, "So that must still hurt." He confirmed, "Oh yeah!"

I started to squat down, and said, "Hold still for just a second. I'm going to pray for you real quick." I put my hand on his ankle, and said, "Right now, in the Name of Jesus, pain go! Ankle, be healed."

I took my hand off his ankle and looked up saying, "Give that a try." He took a few steps, mumbling a "Thank you," as he began to walk away from this unexpected encounter with a stranger. After the first step, his face burst into an expression of shock as he looked back at me in surprise and said, "What???!!!"

I smiled and said, "It's gone isn't it?"

He said, "Yes! That's crazy."

I followed up and said, "Is it completely better, 100 percent?"

He moved a bit and said, "It's not one hundred percent, but it's a huge improvement."

So I said, "Well let me pray once more." After the second prayer, he said that it was completely better with no pain at all.

Then he asked, "Who are you with?" I suppose he was wondering if I was part of a church outreach or something. I said, "I'm with Jesus! I was just waiting here to get my fishing license and saw you walk by."

"No, I mean, what church do you go to. Are you part of a denomination?" I just reiterated, "It's not about one denomination or another. It's about Jesus. He really is the creator God who joined the human race. He's able to heal us, to save us and to make our lives everything He created us to be. He healed your foot today, and He can change your whole life too. Do you know Jesus?"

We had a great discussion about the Lord together. Eventually, I got my fishing license and had a great morning out with my daughter too... even without the coffee!

Living Lessons:

- **You can step out to show God's love no matter how you feel.** God always feels ready. God always "feels spiritual". He doesn't need you to feel a certain way before He'll use you. We are authorized by God to ignore our feelings to obey Him, to believe Him, and to love others. This is more spiritual than any feeling we may have.

- **If you don't see a complete healing instantly, persisting may open the door to an instant miracle.** In this situation, I'm sure he would have been completely happy with a partial healing. By praying a second time, he was completely healed. I see many people healed on a second or third prayer. Don't just quit after one quick prayer. See if you can pray again. Use short prayers of authoritative declarations and test the results often. You'll see more miracles than when you just pray once and walk off.

- **Keep the focus on Jesus, not your church or denomination.**
  God didn't give us miracles to prove our denomination is right or as a gimmick to get people to attend your worship service on Sunday. There is certainly nothing wrong about inviting people to your church. Just be sure

Andy Hayner

to keep the focus on Jesus and be willing to make yourself available for personal follow up.

CHAPTER 3
PARKING LOT REVIVAL

One afternoon I took my family to a small traveling fair in a local parking lot. As we walked around I noticed a man pulling an oxygen tank. As it turned out, it was an old acquaintance of mine from years back named Isaac. Isaac was a large, tall, light skinned black man, but when I saw him today his skin was almost yellow. I asked him what was going on and he told me, "I've got C.O.P.D. They've put me on hospice and say I've only got a couple of months, so I wanted to bring my son out to the fair today." I said, "Well that's not right! I want to pray for your healing right now." I reached my hand and put it on his chest. I said, "Right now, in the Name of Jesus, I command C.O.P.D. to leave him. Lungs, be restored and healed, now! Now, Isaac, take a deep breath and tell me what's happening." He took a big breath… *Cough, hack, wheeze.* So I said, "Don't worry. I'm going to hit this again, because it has to go. In the Name of Jesus, lungs you be healed and restored. All C.O.P.D. leave him now. Take another deep breath Isaac." Isaac breathed in… *Wheeze, cough, hack.* It still hadn't left.

At this point, Isaac was ready to move on with his day at the fair with his son. He said, "Thanks for trying." So I closed up the interaction by saying, "I'm not trying. I'm believing God for your complete recovery. Jesus said, "Believers will lay hands on the sick and they shall recover" so I'm believing you'll be completely restored. Great to see you man. Have a great rest of the day with your son!"

One year later, my wife and I were coming out of Walmart and I noticed a man on the bench just outside the store with a chrome four-pronged cane. So I walked over to him and was surprised to see that it was Isaac sitting there with no oxygen tank and great color. I said, "Isaac! How are you doing man? Where's your oxygen tank?" Isaac exhaled a big puff of his cigarette and said, "Don't need them no more. Jesus healed me!" Wow!

So I asked him about his cane, and he said that he had a bad back and shooting pain through his hip and leg. I said, "Now if Jesus was able to heal your C.O.P.D., do you think He can heal your back and hip?" I laid hands on Isaac and had him test it. He stood up with no pain and walked with no pain. But I noticed a little too much swagger in his stride. So I asked if we could check his alignment. He sat back straight on the bench and I held his legs up in front of him. One of his legs was a clear half inch shorter than the other. So I told him to watch his feet and said, "In the Name of Jesus, short leg grow. Perfect alignment now." His leg immediately shot out until it was even with the other.

I said, "Check it now." Isaac stood up and began walking with a nice, even stride and no pain at all. He bent over, twisted around... still no pain! Out of habit though, he still had his cane in his hand as he walked, but was not using it at all. I told him, "I don't think you'll be needing that cane anymore." Isaac, then lifted the cane above his head, and began saying, "Yah. I don't need this no more!" Then he started to get louder, pumping the cane up and down over his head, "Hey, I don't need this no more. Jesus done healed me!" In his excitement, he started shouting and pumping his cane above his head.

At this point, the sight of a large man swinging a metal bar above his head and shouting in front of Walmart began to gather some onlookers. Some were afraid to come too close and were pausing on their way in, while others did the same thing on their way out. And here's Isaac, still shouting, "Jesus just healed me! I'm healed! I don't need this cane no more" So I joined in the fun and raised my voice, "I just prayed for my friend Isaac, and God healed his back... while he was smoking a cigarette! So I want you to know that Jesus is real. He loves you. He's ready to take you as you are and change your life. Is there anyone here that has any pain or sickness in your body? I want to pray for you right now, real quick and Jesus will heal you too! Don't worry about what you believe or how you think you've been living. This isn't a religious thing. This is about God's love for you. So if you have pain or sickness we want to pray for you real quick. Who has pain or sickness? Anything at all?" Then the Kingdom ministry continued for another 20 minutes right in front of Walmart.

And all this started a year earlier with a man walking away, still pulling his oxygen behind him *after* we had prayed for him.

Living Lessons:
- **God can do huge things even when it looks like nothing happened.** This mini revival began with a "looks like nothing happened" encounter a year earlier.

Andy Hayner

- **Take each encounter as far as there is grace for the interaction.** The first time I met Isaac, he seemed ready to move on after I prayed twice even though had not yet experienced any tangible results. I sent him on with grace and blessing. A year later, he was glad to see me again. This time, when he was instantly healed, he began drawing a crowd. So I lifted up my voice to speak to the crowd.

- **Healing is by grace.** I can't imagine anything more stupid than to go back to smoking cigarettes after you've been healed miraculously of C.O.P.D. (unless of course it is sinning after you've been saved from sin by Jesus Christ. Healing is by grace). We don't judge. We don't criticize. We minister the Kingdom.

- **We can set people free, but for them to stay free, they need to walk in the Kingdom for themselves.** We can set people free by the authority and power we have in the Kingdom. But they need to come to Jesus and walk as His disciples if they are going to stay free. We must heal the sick and proclaim the Kingdom.

- **When you walk in the Kingdom, "amazing" becomes normal.** We were just shopping. God had a revival planned. Wherever you go, you bring the Kingdom... IF you are willing to walk like an ambassador of Christ.

CHAPTER 4
EARS TO HEAR

On a recent mission trip, while walking to the market from my hotel, a young Muslim man began to speak to us in English. He was a seaman by trade but was in port for several weeks. We spoke for a while, so before I left I asked him if he had anything that gave him any pain or problems in his health. He told me that he was very concerned about his ear. Eight weeks earlier he suddenly lost all of his hearing in his ear. He had no idea what had happened and was very concerned that he would be deaf in his ear the rest of his life. I told him that I had seen God heal many people through my prayers, and I would like to lay my hand on his ear to pray for his hearing to be restored. He agreed. Three times I said, "In the Name of Jesus Christ, you deaf spirit, come out now. Ear, be healed and whole. Hear." But each time we checked, he said, "I'm sorry. It is still the same." So after the third time, I wrapped up the interaction by telling him that I will continue to believe that God will heal his ear quickly.

There was a large part of me that was tempted to be disappointed. After all, this had been an obvious "divine appointment" with an English speaking Muslim in a foreign land. This man was obviously open to experiencing the power of God in Jesus Christ. I had stepped out, laid hands expecting a miracle and nothing perceptible happened. But I knew better than to agree with the temptation to be disappointed. Instead, I stirred myself to rejoice in the Lord and give thanks to Him. "Thank you Jesus for the privilege of representing heaven on the earth. Thank You that You are faithful to stand by the gospel with your power and that signs follow me wherever I go. Thank

Andy Hayner

You for opening the door for this ministry. Thank You that believers will lay hands on the sick and they *will* recover. I thank You in advance that this man *will* recover his hearing."

Two days later, I was walking again in the same part of town and I heard someone behind me calling my name. It was this same man. He was jogging towards me with a big smile. "Mr. Andrew. My ear. It is well now! It is well! I woke the next morning after you had prayed and it was well." "Completely?" I asked. He said, "Yes. It is perfect." So we had a nice little chat about how God showed His love for us in Jesus Christ.

What would have happened if we hadn't have bumped into one another that second day? The man would still have been healed, but I would have *never* known about it. So it was right for me to rejoice and thank God by faith in advance. What if a large part of our ministry is like this? Will we allow faith in God's word to encourage us to persist in love and faith, or do we "need to see something" to affirm our faith?

Living Lessons:
- Just because "nothing happened" doesn't mean that "nothing happened. Nothing *never* happens…unless you do nothing. But if you will step out in faith, God's power is always released, always accomplishing the work of the Kingdom of God. Just believe the Word of God, do what it says, and expect God to do His work.

- Don't exchange your faith in God's Word for faith in what your eyes see. Continue to thank God and praise Him by faith according to His Word. Expect God to continue to work and give God time. If necessary, keep reinforcing your faith, but don't draw back or back down.

CHAPTER 5
RISE UP AND WALK

A couple of years ago, I was invited by a pastor to come and pray for a young man, Spencer. Spencer had been run over by a tractor and lived in the pastor's same town. From what I understood, Spencer was sitting on the wheel cover of the tractor while it was in operation and came off of it only to wind up with his middle underneath the tractor tire. Spenser had five major bones shattered— both hips, the pelvis bones, and two lower vertebrae.

The pastor had arranged for me to come over to the house for prayer, so we pulled up to farm house about ten a.m. We walked into the living room, where Spenser's hospital bed and wheel chair had taken over the center of the house.

The entire family had gathered to greet us and watch— dad, mom, brother, sister, and girlfriend. Just in case that wasn't enough onlookers, Spenser's grandmother pulled into the drive just as we began to introduce ourselves to one another.

As we introduced ourselves, we learned that Spenser was unable to move the lower half of his body except by pulling his legs around with his own hands and arms. This was very difficult and painful. He had numbness, shooting pain, and constant dull pain. There was a great deal of uncertainty if Spenser would ever walk again, or whether he would be in pain for the rest of his life. The concern and weariness that hung in the air was even more palpable than the lingering smell of urine from the catheter bag hanging on a hook on the side of Spenser's bed.

As Spenser's grandmother entered the room, she shook my hand, and said ever so sweetly, "It's so nice of you come here and pray." But something in her tone of voice and demeanor made me feel like she was assuming that nothing special was going to happen. In her mind, we were just there to show support for the family, like a religious Hallmark card. I felt it was important for me to rise above that expectation so I spoke up, "I'm glad to be here, but my job isn't to just show support for your family. My job is to freak Spencer's doctors out and get Spenser healed today."

With that, I explained a little more about what Jesus has done to accomplish our healing. Then I laid my hands on Spenser's hips and believed God for his healing. After a few minutes, I asked Spenser to check out his mobility and tell me what he noticed. He immediately pulled his legs up to a forty-five degree angle on his bed without using his hands or arms, prompting several of Spenser's family members to gasp and then begin to cry. I invited my pastor friend, his wife, and my son to also lay hands on Spenser, which took less than ten minutes.

When they were finished I asked Spenser, "Are you ready?" He looked at me and said, "Ready for what?" I said, "To get out of that bed and walk!" He immediately began to make his move, pulling his torso upright with an overhanging "pull up bar", and then he swung his legs off the side of the bed without using his hands or arms. I asked, "How are you feeling?" Spenser responded with a smile, "I feel good." "Any pain?" I asked. He said, "No. I'm feeling good."

His mother had brought over a four pronged walker that Spenser had been unable to use for anything more than bracing to assist maneuvering himself into a wheelchair. With the walker positioned in front of him, Spenser stood straight up on his feet beside the bed without even touching the walker. So I pulled the walker out of his way so that Spenser could walk. He took three steps away from the bed completely unassisted as his family cried, cheered, and clapped! Spenser then returned to his bed, and said, "I don't have any pain, but I still feel a little wobbly." So Spenser continued sitting perfectly upright with his legs hanging over the bed as we talked with the family.

At this point, I shared with the whole family, "It's obvious to see from your reaction that God has done a real miracle here today. I'm not sure where each of you are in your personal faith, but I would say this would be a good time for each of us to get right with God. He's so good. He sent Jesus to be our Savior and Lord, by living for us a perfect life, dying for our sin, and rising from the dead. He's alive and real. He loves you and wants to forgive you and make your life brand new." At that point, I led everyone in the room to call on Jesus for salvation.

The next day I received an update from the pastor. He had seen someone who was with us at Spenser's home in his neighborhood that morning. He asked them, "So how was Spenser after we left?" "Guess what they said," the pastor said to me. I could tell from the pastor's tone of voice, it must be good. He went on to say, "They told me that Spenser went out riding his Gator (like a four wheeler designed like a flatbed truck) around the farm for *three hours that afternoon* with absolutely no pain!" Praise Jesus!

Living Lessons:

- **Nothing is too difficult for God!** God makes bones, organs, and perfectly whole bodies starting with just a few living cells every day. Perfect wholeness is in the Name of Jesus.

- **Contradict doubt, unbelief, and low expectations by proclaiming the good news of Jesus and what He can do.** This is not depending upon the faith of others. This is not allowing the unbelief of others to influence you into living down to the level of their low expectations. I didn't need to get "all the unbelief out of the room", but I did need to keep the unbelief in the room from influencing me or my team.

- **God's okay with you putting Him on the spot for things that demonstrate His love and advance His Kingdom.** We let everyone know that we were not there for condolences and well wishes. We were there to see a young man get out of bed and walk. We put God on the spot by speaking out our expectations of God. Then we put our faith into action. God did all the rest.

CHAPTER 6
RACE YOU TO THE CAR

A couple of years ago I was attending a Christian conference when some good friends of mine tapped me on the shoulder, "Andy, we need you." As I started walking towards the back of the room my friends told me, "There's a little girl who can't walk. Her parents brought her here for healing." They didn't come to get me because I had some 'special healing anointing.' They came to get me because they knew I have a heart for children and a gift to help them feel at ease as we are ministering to them.

When I got towards the back of the room, I was introduced to Anya. She was seven years old and was born with cerebral palsy. She was a very sweet little girl, but physically weak and unable to stand without leaning on something, and unable to walk more than a step or two without falling. She also suffered from regular seizures.

We began to lay hands on Anya and exercise the authority and power of the Kingdom of God for her healing. There were about three of us who took the lead in ministering to Anya. We worked as a team, with each of us taking turns for a few minutes, then stepping away and allowing the next one to continue to release the power of the Holy Spirit into Anya's body for healing. We also periodically stopped and told Anya, "Let's walk now, and see how you are doing." We kept this up for close to thirty minutes with little visible results.

Amazing Healing Encounters

I still remember the hotel manager watching us with a condescending smirk as the name of "Jesus" reverberated through the conference hotel lobby as we ministered to Anya. But his smirk changed to astonishment when this precious little girl began walking freely and even running around in the hotel lobby! Anya's healing made a huge surge forward that evening.

Everyone was so excited to see the joy on Anya's face as she walked and played games to continue exercise her new found strength and coordination! She left the hotel lobby with an over the shoulder mischievous glance at her parents saying, "Race you to the car!" That evening, after she got home, she ran around in the backyard with her brother and sisters—something she had never been able to do before! Anya has remained free from seizures for the past two years and has continued to walk strong forwards, backwards, and sideways, including up and down stairs. Praise the Lord!

Living Lessons:
- **God heals birth defects. He doesn't cause them.** Jesus healed people who were lame, blind, and deaf since birth. Just because we are born with certain conditions, doesn't mean that this is God's intention for us. We were born sinners. Yet God makes us new through Christ.

- **Persistence pays off.** The promises of God are inherited through "faith *and perseverance*". Faith is not a moment of trust to get what we want from God. It's a permanent posture of the heart that directs our entire lifestyle because we've seen who God is in Jesus Christ.

- **Teamwork among like-minded Kingdom believers can help you persist beyond what you may be able to do alone.** If you've been getting worn down by the enemy, turn your battle into a tag-team match.

- **God is often multi-tasking.** I was primarily focused on ministering to Anya. However, I'm sure that God was also ministering to the hotel manager and others that may have observed this miracle.

CHAPTER 7
NO MORE JINX

One afternoon, several of my friends set aside some time together to go into the city to touch people with the love of the Kingdom. After we were finished, we gathered back at our house for some pizza and fellowship. I was sent to the grocery store to pick up some drinks and paper plates.

One of the young ladies who had gone out with another group asked if she could come with me to the store. As we walked through the store, I saw a few people that needed ministry, so I started conversations and asked them if my friend could pray for them. After she prayed for a third person, she looked at me and said, "I must be some sort of jinx or something!" I said, "Huh?" She continued, "I just mean that I'm not seeing any BANG BOOM miracles, and I want to see miracles!"

Although I was excited about her zeal, I felt compelled to address something. I said, "First of all, you are not a jinx. You are a daughter of the living God and an ambassador of His Kingdom. Second, stop trying to get your identity from your ministry results. We don't need miracles to happen to make ourselves feel affirmed. We want miracles for the people who are hurting and for the glory of God."

We turned to go and check out and hadn't walked more than ten steps when I saw a lady who was bent over pushing a shopping cart with a walker inside of it. Her husband was with her so I decided to speak to her husband first. I said, "How are you today? I noticed your wife's walker. Is she in pain?" He told me a little about his wife's condition. Then I said, "Wow! Today is your lucky day! My friends has a ministry of praying for people and seeing them healed. You should let her pray for your wife real quick." He responded, "Well my hip is in terrible pain." Chivalry at its finest.

I said to the husband, "Great. Then I'll pray for you and my friend can pray for your wife."

As we asked a little more, the wife said, "Not only do I have pain in my back, my bones are a mess. So this is actually as far up as I can go." While I ministered to the husband, my friend, who had just called herself a jinx, laid hands on this lady. The husband said, "It's gone!" He was healed. Then the lady said, "I felt something when you prayed! Your hand was getting really warm and now my back is tingling." She wasn't completely healed yet when she tested it, so my friend prayed a second time. This time my friend said, "Can you feel that?" Bones were shifting under my friends' hand as she prayed. The then lady stood up straight and said, "My bones! Oh my, this is strange!" All pain was gone. She was able to stand up straight with no issues. She was completely healed. God had healed her back through my friend.

Living Lessons:

- **We don't get our identity from miracles. Miracles come from our identity!** We don't look to miracles to tell us that we are children of God. The word of God tells us that! We don't heal so that we can prove ourselves. We are free from all that. Our identity is established in the unshakable union we have with Jesus Christ. As we walk in this, God's power and love flows through us and people are blessed.

- **Hands on discipleship plays an important role in helping us move past our barriers.** This young lady needed help to begin to live the life she believed God wanted to live through her. We all do. Who are you helping? Who are you seeking help from?

CHAPTER 8
NO THANK YOU… I CHANGED MY MIND

My oldest daughter, Noel, is the quiet type. She's the middle child. She likes playing piano, reading, riding horses, and hanging out with a few friends. You'd never expect that she'd be so amazing, but she is. She walks in the love and power of God.

One afternoon, I had taken my family and some friends to a farmer's market. My oldest daughter, Noel, who was about thirteen years old at the time, saw a lady with a four-pronged cane who was sitting on a bench near the sidewalk. I watched her as she walked over to the lady and said, "Hi! How are you today? I noticed that you were sitting here with a cane and wondered if you have pain when you walk." The lady responded, "Oh yes dear. I'm an old lady. When you get my age you'll have pain when you walk too." To which my daughter smiled and said, "No I won't. But I would sure like to pray for you. I've seen God heal lots of people and I know that He loves you."

The lady's countenance soured immediately and she drew back. She abruptly said, "No thank you. I don't believe in God."

My daughter remained pleasant and undeterred. With a smile and pleasant tone, she said, "That's okay. It'll still work because I believe."

At this point the lady stopped being polite. She said, "I said no! Now please let me alone."

So my daughter, continuing to smile, peacefully waved goodbye and said, "Okay. I hope you have a great day!"

My daughter rejoined us and we walked on and prayed for some others.

Let me pause here to say that, in my experience, this is the place where many believers who are new to walking in the fullness of Jesus Christ begin to feel deflated. You had the courage to approach someone in love and they turned you down flat. Do you feel like a failure? I want to tell you, you absolutely have NOT failed.

Let's pick up with the rest of this story.

About twenty minutes or so later, we were passing back by the same bench and the same lady with the four-pronged cane spotted my daughter passing by. She got up off her bench and walked over to my daughter and said, "Hi there. I'm so glad I saw you again. I just wanted to say that it was very kind of you to take notice of me and offer to pray for me, and I had no cause to be rude to you. What you did was very kind and positive. Even though I don't believe in God, it surely won't hurt. So if you'd like to pray for me, I believe I'll take that prayer now."

Apparently, even though my daughter's initial interaction had not turned out the way we had hoped, the Holy Spirit had used the very act of approaching her in God's love to begin to deal with this lady's conscience.

The best part was that as my daughter prayed for the lady, her hip pain decreased significantly immediately. My daughter introduced me (since I was now walking with her) so we prayed together for the lady a second time and the hip pain was dramatically reduced yet again. Now the lady was standing there stunned with her mouth open in shock. I took the opportunity to share with her, "Ma'am, I know there are a lot of mean and hypocritical people who claim to be Christians. I want to let you know that Jesus Christ isn't like that. He's real. He's loving, kind and merciful, and everything He ever did He did for you. He wants to forgive you and heal you and be with you forever." At this point, she gave me a huge hug and began to weep on my shoulder before she walked away. All of this started with manifesting grace and redemptive love in the face of rudeness and rejection!

Living Lessons:
- **God is able to manifest Himself through us in the mere act of approaching people with love and faith.** The peace and kindness of my daughter created a divine impression on this lady that spoke to her.

- **It's NOT about never being rejected. It's about never letting fear of rejection stop you.**

- **The way we handle rejection is part of manifesting Christ in this world. God can speak to people through us, even if they reject us, if we handle it in the grace of Christ.** Just as God has used the way that Jesus Christ suffered to reveal Himself to many people, God will use us when we encounter rejection in the power of His Spirit to convict others.

- **God is able to use our differences in personalities to the advantage of the Kingdom.** My daughter's quiet and steady personality was the perfect tool for God to reach this lady with the gospel. This lady may not have felt as bad about her attitude had it been directed towards me, a full grown man. But the Holy Spirit flowing through the tenderness and pleasant demeanor of my daughter, Noel, was the perfect recipe to soften this lady's heart.

CHAPTER 9
METAL KNEE

"God can do anything He wants!" We say it, but do we really believe it when He does something that breaks all the "laws" of science and every attempt at a human explanation?

I was once ministering the Word of God at a conference when I young man approached me on the break. He asked if I would be willing to pray for his knee. He pointed out the large zipper-like scar running alongside his knee.

He wasn't sure he was allowed to ask for prayer because he had already had knee surgery. "Can you pray for that?" he asked. He explained that he had a snowboarding injury a couple of years earlier, but his knee still caused him a lot of pain, especially when he walked on it.

I had him sit down on the chair and put my hands on his knee, saying, "Knee be healed. Be new. Everything causing pain, go now."

Now, I don't usually feel anything when I pray for people. I'm not prone to tingles and shivers or the like. I've had people fall over under the power of God and others begin to tremble shouting that they feel fire coming from my hands, while all the while I feel nothing. I don't mind. I don't operate by sensations. I operate by faith in Jesus Christ.

However, in this particular instance, as I laid hands on this young man's knee, I began to feel what seemed to be like invisible liquid heat funneling out of my hands directly into this young man's knee. Because this sensation was so obvious, it alerted me to the fact that the Holy Spirit's work was definitely under way. This sensation continued for around two minutes, so I just left my hands on his knee, allowing God to do whatever He was doing, not completely understanding what I was sensing or why.

When this sensation subsided, I asked the young man to check out his knee by doing something he couldn't do before. So he stood up and began to squat down and stand back up several times. He smiled and said that for the first time since his injury he had no pain at all in his knee. What the doctors couldn't fix with all their scalpels, screws, pins, and titanium, King Jesus fixed in less than two minutes.

While that would be a wonderful miracle in and of itself, it's fairly common place. What made this one of my favorite miracles was to be disclosed two days later.

On the final session of the conference, I opened the meeting up for anyone who wanted to share a testimony to encourage those who were there. This young man came up to share.

As I handed him the microphone, he said, "As many of you already no, I messed up my knee really bad a couple of years ago in a snowboarding accident. Even after surgery, I had a lot of pain in it. After prayer, I've not had any pain now for two day for the first time since my accident."

Everyone began to clap, and I reached for the microphone thinking he was finished. But then he continued, "But that's not all. When I had my surgery, they actually gave me an artificial knee that was held together with screws and pins. I could feel the tips of some of these screws and pins through the skin. I had a nervous habit of messing with them whenever I sat down with shorts. I say "HAD" a habit because ever since I received prayer, the pins and screws are GONE! My artificial knee feels just like the other one now— no screws, no pins, no metal corners. It's just like the other one now!"

God had given this young man a brand new knee. I have no idea what happened to the titanium one. It's just gone. Wow!

Living Lessons:
- **You don't need to feel anything. Just obey by faith in God's Word.** If the Holy Spirit does cause you to feel something, just pay attention and cooperate. Otherwise, assume the Holy Spirit thinks you're doing just fine without it and carry on.

- **God is able to make all things new (yes, even when it breaks the "laws" of science.)** "When you believe, NOTHING shall be impossible for you." (Mt. 17:20)

CHAPTER 10
NO LONGER KNOWN BY THE SCARS

People need healing for many different reasons. Sometimes people are born with certain conditions. Others were injured in an accident. While yet others are attacked by a disease of some sort. Once people learn that Jesus Christ suffered stripes on His back specifically to purchase healing for our physical bodies, they freely begin to believe God's grace for the healing of these afflictions.

However, in my ministry, I've observed that there is a subset of issues that people often question whether God's supernatural healing applies. One of these is the area of self-inflicted health issues. For some reason people hesitate to believe that God's grace for healing would apply equally to things that are caused by their own actions such as sexually transmitted diseases, hepatitis contracted through drug use, scars caused by self-mutilation, and so on.

Jesus said, "The thief comes to steal, to kill, and to destroy..." (John 10:10). Satan steals what he knows does not belong to him. He steals our God-given destiny and value. He destroys our relationships and our health. How? While there are a number of devices at Satan's disposal in this world, one of his main tools is deception. As we walk around in the darkness, people often hurt themselves.

I met one such girl as I was ministering in a Christian residential recovery program. She approached me on a break and asked me about her arms. She said, "Can God heal me of this?" She rolled up her shirt sleeves to reveal her forearms, thickly spotted with deep burgundy burn marks. "I used to burn myself with cigarettes."

Without hesitation I replied, "I know He can. He's already paid for it sweetie. He's just waiting on you to receive it."
She shared her hesitation, "I've just been told that I'd have to live with the consequences of my bad decisions. So I wasn't sure."

I replied, "Did God forgive you of all the sins you committed while you were walking in darkness and deception?"

She said, "Yes."

I continued, "So if God has forgiven you of the sin and isn't holding that against you at all, what would hold Him back from healing you? It's certainly not God."

I could see the light of hope come across her face. But I wanted to drive the point home even further. "When you were living apart from Christ, you probably experienced a lot of things that caused you a lot of emotional turmoil, right?" She nodded. "Yet, you know that God doesn't want you carrying that baggage around in your heart. He wants to heal your heart and set you free from all the junk that Satan put in your heart, right? Or is God just going to leave you with all that stuff as the consequences of your choices?"

"No, He's healing me and setting me free," she responded.

Looking her in the eye, very deliberately I said, "If God will heal your heart, why wouldn't He heal your body too? What makes that any different? The same lifestyle that hurt your heart is the same lifestyle that hurt your body. The same Jesus that paid to give you a new heart also paid a high price to heal your body."

She chuckled with relief and exclaimed, "Well, all right! Then let's get these ugly marks off of me."

I gripped both of her forearms in my hands and said, "In the Name of Jesus Christ, skin become new. All damaged tissue, be healed. Perfect skin. She's forgiven of all her sin, and healed by the stripes of Jesus Christ."

When I was finished, she took a quick glance at her arms as did I. There was no noticeable change. So I encouraged her, "Let's believe God to make your arms new. Meanwhile, don't worry at all about what you see. By faith, each day just thank God for your healing. Consider it done. It's happening. Just give God time." She agreed.

Around six months later, I returned to that same ministry for another conference. This same young lady was there. Now she was a counselor in the program, helping the new participants get established in their recovery and transformation.

She met me at the back of the room as I was setting up for the conference. Excitedly she pulled up her shirt sleeves and said, "Check this out!" Her arms were healed! All of the scars from her dark season of self-inflicted cigarette burns had disappeared!

Andy Hayner

No more would she have to deal with a constant reminder of the darkest days and worst decisions of her life. Jesus had made her new, inside and out.

Living Lessons:
- Healing is by grace through the stripes of Jesus Christ. Don't limit God's ability to overcome the work of the enemy, even if we were complicit at one time.

- God is willing and able to heal us from even those things that were caused by our own bad decisions.

- If healing doesn't take place instantly, remain in faith considering it done even before you see the manifested results.

CHAPTER 11
THE GREEN HAIRED MAN

Since discovering that the power of God will work through any believer, I have made it a large part of my ministry to disciple people to walk in the fullness of Jesus Christ wherever they go. For me, this involves helping people to experience how they can advance the kingdom of God by ministering to people out on the streets.

One afternoon I had taken a couple of people to a college campus to see if we could meet some students and show them God's love. We wandered over to the student center where I approached a group of about five students coming out of the building.

"Hey, would you guys like to see something cool?" I asked with a grin. They halted their journey to see what this stranger may have to show them. "Sure, I guess," one of them responded.

I asked, "So which of you have something that gives you pain, like an injury that didn't heal, or something that gives you issues that you're just living with now?" One young man spoke up, "I've got a really bad knee. It hurts me all the time when I walk on it."

"Cool. I want to show you something. I want you to stand still. I'm going to put my hand on your knee for a second and you'll see something really cool." So he obliged as all his friends gathered in to see what I was going to do.

I leaned down and put my finger tips to his knee and said, "Right now, in the Name of Jesus Christ, knee be completely healed. All pain come out." Then I stood up and told the student, "Now move around and tell me how your knee feels. I want you to be completely honest." He said, "Oh I will."

As he squatted down and stood back up, a look of shock came over his face. "No way!!" he exclaimed. Then he repeated the motion a couple of more times, talking to his friends, "This is crazy. It's gone. I've had this my whole life."

I began to ask his friends, "Do you think your friend is for real? Or is he just lying to all of you to make me feel better?" They chuckled, "No, he's telling the truth." I then began to ask them, "Do you know how this happened?" And from there I shared the gospel of Jesus Christ with them.

As we went our separate ways, I began to look for our next opportunity and noticed a young man with green hair sitting on a bench not far away. He apparently had been watching us but forgot that he was staring at us. So when he noticed that I was looking in his direction, he immediately turned away with a bit of a look that I interpreted as, "I'm not sure what you're doing buddy, but whatever it is, don't bring it over here."

Whether that was the vibe he truly intended to give off or not, I'm not sure, but it's how his body language spoke to me.

So what did I do? I balked. I decided to walk on by and to look for someone who looked "more receptive". The crazy thing was that, whereas a few minutes ago there were swarms of people, now there wasn't anyone around. The whole campus had become a ghost town. I looked across the street… nope, no one there. I looked left, then right. Classes had started. Everyone else was gone.

With the green-haired man as our only immediate opportunity, and that looking "not so promising", my partners and I did what most people do in situations like this… we started chit chatting amongst ourselves.

The Holy Spirit decided to interrupt the chit chat by speaking to my heart, "What are you doing?" He inquired.

"Chickening out" I thought.

The Holy Spirit didn't like that reply. He said, "No you are not!"

Gulp.

The Holy Spirit continued, "If he's going to reject you, why don't you just make him man up and do it. How's that going to hurt you? Why don't you go over and overcome evil with good. Poor out some acceptance on his rejection and see what happens."

God had shifted my heart. I wasn't going to allow fear of rejection keep me from advancing the Kingdom of God. How can I be rejected when God has accepted me?

I said to my buddies, "Hey guys. Let's go over and talk to that guy."

I started over to the guy with the green hair. He was now joined by a young lady. He sat with ear buds in his ears, face fixed on the screen of his smart phone. As I approached, he looked up and noticed me coming towards him. It was now obvious that I was approaching him, so he dropped one of his ear buds out (just one... signaling he didn't intend for this to be a long conversation requiring two ears).

I smiled at him and said, "I noticed your hair and just wanted to say that I really like it. I'll bet you get a lot of comments." He rolled his eyes and said, "Yah, a few."

Before you judge me ("Come on! You don't really like green hair. You liar") you need to understand, in all honesty, I decided to like green hair at that very moment. I can do that. We all can. We are free to decide to show people favor and acceptance all we want. My guess is that anyone who will dye their hair bright green is probably looking for a little attention. Why not show a little interest to someone in whom God is extremely interested? That's called "grace". We're allowed to show it!

Then I took our interaction to the next level. I pulled off my cowboy hat exposing my balding head, and said, "Truth is, I'm jealous!" We both laughed a bit and a big smile broke out on the young man's face. The ice had been broken.

The Holy Spirit had done it. He broke through rejection with God's grace. He had also broken through my fears and prejudices to fill my heart with grace and a willingness to risk rejection for the sake of showing God's love to a stranger.

Now, I walked through the open door, "Hey, I can see you're just hanging out and wanted to see if there was anything you might need prayer for. My buddies and I decided to come out and just pray for folks today. We're not doing background checks to see who's been naughty and whose been nice. In fact God just healed a guys knee right over there. So if you have any health issues, or anything else, we'd love to pray for you."

He sat back and said, "Well, actually I'm feeling pretty good. I'm pretty healthy honestly." He paused, but then continued, "But do you guys pray for depression?" This was quickly moving towards becoming a "two-eared conversation."

When you bring the Kingdom of God, you're not a "one-trick-pony." Healing is just one expression of the power of God's Kingdom to set captives free from the oppression of the enemy.

"Sure we can pray for depression. God doesn't want you depressed. He made us to live in His peace and joy."

I decided to enquire a little about his depression. "Sometimes when people get really depressed, they can feel it, like they could almost put their hand on it— like in their gut, or their chest. When you get really depressed, can you feel it?"

He said, "Yes. I feel it in my head."

Andy Hayner

This wasn't my normal approach and I don't think it's necessary. It's just the way this conversation went on that day.

I asked, "I'd like to put my hand on the side of your head then while I pray for you, because I believe God is going to shift things for you and take this depression out of you right now." As he nodded his permission, I moved around to stand beside him while placing my hand gently on the side of his head.

Then I began addressing his depression. "In the Name of Jesus Christ, depression and everything causing it, you go from him right now. Loose him. I set him free. I release peace. Fill Him with peace right now Holy Spirit."

As I was speaking, I noticed that the countenance of the young man had changed. His eyes were closed and he had a peaceful grin on his face, like he was just about to giggle. After a short while, I paused and asked, "What's happening?"

He said, "I'm not sure, but it's good!"

At this point the Holy Spirit spoke the word, "Witchcraft" to my heart. So, to confirm this word, I enquired of the young man, "There are a lot of approaches to spirituality and spiritual power and lots of them aren't connected with Jesus Christ. Have you been involved in some of this stuff?"

He replied, "Yes, and actually I've been wondering if that didn't have something to do with making my depression worse."

Then I said, "I believe it does. That's probably why the Lord had me ask you about it. So I guess the question is whether or not you're willing to give that stuff up and turn your life over to Jesus."

He said, "Yes, absolutely."

I then took a more aggressive stance focused specifically against demonic powers at work in his life by addressing them directly. I said, "In the Name of Jesus Christ, I take authority over every unclean spirit at work in His life. He belongs to Jesus. Now Go! Come out and never return." As I did so, he jolted like electricity was going through him, jerking his hands and arms. Eventually he returned to a peaceful state. Then I invited him to pray a prayer of commitment to Jesus Christ and receiving the Holy Spirit.

As you can imagine, this all caught the attention of his female friend who was looking on, which opened up more doors for ministry in her life as well.

All this started with the Holy Spirit giving grace to overcome a "go away" expression and overcome evil with good.

Living Lessons:
- Don't judge people by how they appear. Don't be deterred by how they treat you. View people through the cross of Christ for them and overcome evil with good.

- Fear of rejection is a lie. You are accepted by God and free to love. If God is for you, who can harm you?

- We aren't limited to healing. We have the Kingdom so we can set people free from whatever is oppressing them.

- Part of setting people free is leading them to repentance and faith in Jesus Christ so that they can maintain their freedom.

CHAPTER 12
THE KINGDOM DELIVERED

We tend to make things more complicated than they really are. Often times solutions are very simple. They're just not easy. But our issue usually isn't complicated. It's just difficult. But when things aren't solved easily, we often assume that the solution is complicated, when in fact it may be very simple. It's just not easy.

Nowhere is this more apparent in the body of Christ today than in the area of healing and deliverance. For Jesus and His disciples, healing was a simple matter of the presence of the Kingdom of God exerting it's authority and power to set captives free. No background checks. No long winded prayers. No begging and tears. No complicated formulas or jumping through hoops. It was a simple matter of exercising the authority and power of God by faith.

However, if you walk into any church and request ministry for healing today, many of the mindsets and practices you would experience would be very different. Many prevalent approaches begin with a spiritual background check that rivals the FBI. "What's your spiritual background?" "Have you dealt with all the spiritual open doors in your blood line?" "Have you been naughty or nice? Are you worthy?" "Was your Grandfather a Mason? Oh no, what degree?" This is not the way of the Kingdom demonstrated by Jesus Christ and His disciples.

Andy Hayner

Not long after God taught me about the simplicity of walking in the authority of the Name of Jesus Christ, God allowed me to see just how simple things are in the Kingdom. I was ministering in a bi-lingual church and invited people who needed healing in their bodies to come forward for prayer. A middle aged lady came forward saying that she had constant pain in her one of her knees. So I placed my hand on her knees and spoke in the Name of Jesus, "Right now, knee be healed. Pain go."

Then I had the lady move and test her knee. She reported that there was improvement but not complete relief yet. So I decided to minister again. However, as I ministered this time, rather than merely addressing the knee or getting more specific (which had been my tendency in the past) I felt like I should just focus on believing God for the release of His power for whatever she needed. So I issued a general command in Jesus' Name, "Right now, everything not of God afflicting this lady, GO!"

As soon as I said this, the lady doubled forward and began convulsing wildly. Her eyes had rolled back in her head and she continued to convulse forward in waves. After about thirty seconds, the lady stood up straight and gave a huge guttural belch, sounding more like a linebacker showing off at a drinking party than a lady at a church service.

After she belched, she opened her eyes and relief came across her face. I looked at her and asked, "Are you okay?" She smiled and said, "Yes. I feel lighter and free." We both realized that an unclean spirit had just gone out of her, much to our surprise. We didn't even know she needed to be set free from a demon, much less how the demon got there, or what the demon's name was. We thought this was about her knee getting healed (which did get completely healed too, by the way). As it turned out, it was about the Kingdom of God!

Living Lessons:

- **Healing and deliverance are essentially the same. It's the Kingdom of God setting captives free.** If we believe they are different things, we will limit the flow of God's power through us by our mindsets, kind of like a hose nozzle set on midst verses shower. When we release the Kingdom without restriction, we will see God do many things that go beyond our own understanding.

- **We should take basically the same approach for healing and deliverance. We are exerting the authority and power of the Kingdom of God.** Jesus told his disciples to "heal the sick, and cast out demons" and proclaim, "the Kingdom of heaven is at hand." The approach is the same either way— exerting the authority and power of God by faith to set captives free. If they need freedom in their bodies, this is healing. If they need freedom in their souls from demonic oppression, this is casting out demons.

- **We don't need to do spiritual background checks to set people free.** We don't need to know the cause of diseases or demonic oppression to set people free. Jesus never felt the need to investigate the cause of sicknesses or demonic oppression. He already knew! "*The thief* comes to steal, kill and destroy…" What's important is that we know that God has given us the authority to set people free in Jesus' Name, and that we act in this authority.

- **God will do more for people as we believe Him for things beyond what we can understand.** Don't get bogged down in the details. You don't need to figure out the flesh or the soul. Just stay in the Spirit and operate according to what you see in Jesus Christ. He's all you need.

CHAPTER 13
YOU GET BETTER RESULTS THAN ME

God has blessed me with a wife that is a true woman of God. She walks with Jesus and has made our family her chief labor in the Kingdom. We are all better for it!

On our twentieth wedding anniversary, I was able to take my wife away for a relaxing weekend together. We distributed our children to stay with some trusted friends, and took off. It was great. We were actually able to talk and listen without interruption.

I particularly remember one conversation in which I asked my wife, "So what are your dreams for the next twenty years, and what can I do to help make your dreams come true?" It was during that conversation that we both felt that God had spoken something to our hearts— "build an apostolic family".

While we didn't quite know what that meant, it captured our hearts. What would it look like to raise up a family that was advancing the Kingdom of God with an apostolic revelation of Jesus Christ wherever we went? We weren't sure, but we left that weekend with a renewed sense of destiny from God to live out that vision, a journey we are still on together.

Along that path, we've learned many such lessons together. One powerful lesson took place when my son and I went away to minister at weekend conference.

Andy Hayner

At the end of the first day, I invited people to come forward who wanted prayer for healing in their bodies. Since my son was with me, I invited him to come up to the front to help me pray for people.

As the evening wrapped up, my son and I loaded up the car and pulled away from the conference venue. For me it had been a great evening. God was really moving powerfully. I was curious as to how my son had experienced God at work, so I asked, "How'd it go tonight buddy?"

My son let out a big sigh, "Well Dad, honestly I'm trying not to be discouraged right now."

Well that wasn't what I was expecting. I enquired, "Really? What's up?"

He responded, "I know that I have the same Jesus and the same Holy Spirit that you do, but I just notice that you get better results than I do."

What's a dad to say at times like this? You try to give your children opportunities for amazing experiences that will build their lives, and sometimes it seems to backfire. What I had hoped would encourage him now had him on the ropes, fighting an onslaught of discouragement.

Then the Spirit of God rose up in me with a burst of truth and revelation that cut through the darkness. "Son, I don't get ANY results. And the part of you that is getting discouraged that *you don't get the results* you'd like to see, is probably the same part that would get puffed up and proud if you had walked out of here with tons of miracle testimonies tonight. Because that's the part that believes that *you* have something to do with getting those results."

I paused for a moment to check his reaction and allow him to process what I had said so far. When I could see he was tracking with me and waiting for me to say more, I continued, "So let's make a deal. How about we just let Jesus Christ be the only one who gets any results. It's not you verses me or me verses you. It's just Jesus getting results. Okay?"

Relief came over his face. "Wow! That's perfect. Yes! Jesus is the only one who gets any results." It proved to be a timely word.

The next night we were at a different venue for ministry. So, just as I had done the previous night, at the conclusion of my message I invited people to come forward who wanted prayer for healing. I also invited Simeon to come up and help me pray for people.

As it turned out, Jesus got some amazing results through Simeon that night. One man had burst his ear drum in an industrial accident years earlier. My son laid hands on the man's ear and the man's ear became whole. He began to hear with perfect hearing.

Jesus gets great results, especially when we let ministry be about Him instead of ourselves.

Andy Hayner

Living Lessons:

- **Jesus is the only one who gets results.** We need to look past people whom God is using and see Jesus Christ, the same Jesus Christ who lives in us.

- **We don't get our identity or joy from ministry results. Our identity and our joy is in Jesus Christ!** If we make ministry our source of identity and joy, we will get discouraged (when things go wrong) or get proud (when things go well). We must trust and obey without regard to results we see. When we allow Jesus Christ to be our source of joy and identity, ministry becomes an overflow of love. Ministry results become an opportunity to give thanks and praise instead of a temptation to pride or discouragement.

CHAPTER 14
I FEEL LIKE I CAN PRAY

One night, I found myself driving through a heavy snow storm trying to make it to the city of my next conference. A one hour drive turned into a two and a half hour drive because the condition of the road was so bad.

To make things worse, about half-way through my journey, I began to hear a rhythmic "clump, swish, clump, swish…" as one of my windshield wipers had accumulated enough snow and wiper fluid to become a motorized ice hammer smacking into the edges of the car frame. Turning the wipers off wasn't an option in those weather conditions, so I pressed on, ignoring the racket… that is until the "clump, swish, clump" turned into an awful "skreeeeeeetch, skreeeeeetch."

Apparently windshield wipers are not designed to bear an additional twenty pounds of ice. Finally, my wiper had broken off completely, leaving only the metal wiper mounting bar to scrape back and forth directly on the glass of my windshield. I was amazed at how similar this sound was to someone scraping their finger nails down a chalk board. It was so terrible, I tried to turn off the wipers, but quickly realized that it was more important to see than to maintain my sanity. So back on went the wipers. The maddening skreeetching continued and continued… and continued.

Andy Hayner

Thankfully, about an hour later I arrived safely at my destination ready for a good night's rest. Quiet never sounded so good.

The next morning on the way into the conference, I decided to pull into an oil change station to pick up some new wipers. I asked the attendant if he had replacement wipers, preferably some that were capable of withstanding an additional twenty pounds of ice and snow.

As he passed me a clipboard to fill out my contact information, I noticed he had some fairly substantial tattoos on his forearms. I commented, "Hey man, those are some cool tats."

He said, "Thanks. You really like them?" holding his arms out to me for a closer look.

I said, "Yeah, these are really cool." One of the most prominent features of his tattoo was a brick wall. I asked, "Those are amazing. Have you ever thought about adding some red highlights into the bricks of the wall? Since your skin is so dark, it'd probably look like real bricks. That might really make it pop even more."

His face lit up, "Oh man. I've been telling my friends I'm going to do that. They're saying no, but I think like you, man. That settles it now."

A friend had been made. No longer was this guy just my "windshield wiper guy". We had connected as real people. The simple act of taking notice of people, things that might be important to them, and entering into their lives with grace and kindness had made another stranger a friend.

As he got the details of my wiper measurements, I asked him, "How's your body holding up in the cold these days? Lots of people have injuries that give them issues, especially when it turns off cold. How about you?"

He said, "I'm doing alright."

Something about the way he responded didn't sit well with me. It gave me the impression that he was pushing through the pain without complaining.

So I pushed a little further, "So you're not dealing with *any* pain or injuries?"

He opened up a little more, "Not really. I got a bad back injury when I played football in high school, but it's nothing I can't live with."

He left the oil change bay to go into the office and retrieve my wipers, so I decided to get out of my car and follow him inside. He was coming out with my wipers just as I met him at the door. I said, "Hey, while you're up, let me help you with something really quick. Let's check the alignment in your back. Since you've been injured, even if it's not causing you a lot of grief now, as you get older it could, if your alignment is off."

He walked with me back into the office and I instructed him to sit in a chair pressing his hips squarely back in the chair. He

Andy Hayner

complied. Then I told him to relax his legs as I picked them up in front of him. As I held his feet together with his legs extended, it was immediately apparent that his right leg was a full inch shorter than the left one. I pointed this out to my new friend, and he confessed that he already knew about that.

At this point, I'm sure this guy probably thought I was just a friendly chiropractor who was going to pop his neck or something. Boy, was he in for a suprise!

As he sat there with me holding his feet together out in front of him, I said, "Watch this. In the Name of Jesus Christ, I command that the power of God go through His body and bring him back into alignment. Be healed now!" As I said this, the bones in his body shifted and his right foot came out to be perfectly even with the other.

I looked up at his face and asked, "What did you feel?" He looked at me with a completely dumbfounded look on his face that quickly curled up into an uncontrollable outburst of tears. He buried his face into his hands and began saying, "Oh man. Oh man. It just went right through me. Oh man."

At this point, I realized that one of his co-workers had walked in and been watching this whole event unfold. So I stood up and positioned myself between them as a bit of a shield to protect my new friend from any potential shame while he collected himself. I then began to speak with them both about Jesus Christ, His power, His presence, and His death on the cross and resurrection.

I invited them both to receive Christ, and the young man who was healed prayed right then and there to receive Jesus Christ as Savior and Lord.

Afterward, he began to share his back story with me. He said, "You just don't know. My whole life has been so hard. My friends would always tell me, `You just need to pray.' But I would always tell them, `Why? What good does it do?' I wasn't trying to be disrespectful or nothing. I had just tried praying before and I felt so fake. I felt like I was pretending and speaking to the air."

He continued, "And just last night, I was going through some YouTube videos and somehow got into some videos about God. I watched a few of them and said, `I don't know if God real or not, but if He is, I hope He comes to get me because I'm really missing out if this stuff is real.'" Then he started to tear up again as he said, "I know he did this for me! Wow! Now I know I can pray! For the first time in my life, I know God is real. I can pray now!"

And there we stood in the middle of the oil change garage, two men who had been complete strangers less than ten minutes ago, one young black man crying like a baby as he embraced a middle aged white man. That's the Kingdom of God!

Living Lessons:
- **You can make friends for the sake of the Kingdom by showing grace to strangers.** This is no "canned conversion" quest. This is interacting with people out of the heart of Jesus Christ. While some people might judge

Andy Hayner

people for their tattoos, you can use anything as an opportunity to get to know people and show them grace.

- **God is working in the lives of the people you meet every day.** Adopt the mindset that every place you go, you are God's ambassador ready to bring people face to face with the living God. Every interaction is a divine appointment when you seek first the Kingdom. God wants to encounter people through you.

WHO WILL YOU MEET TODAY?

WHAT CAN YOU DO TO SHOW THE PEOPLE YOU MEET THE LOVE AND POWER OF GOD?

ADDITIONAL RESOURCES FROM THE AUTHOR

You will find additional resources from Andy Hayner at his ministry website **FullSpeedImpact.com**.

If you want to learn how to experience the power of your identity in Christ, *Your Place in the Son* is the book for you. You will see the reality of your union with Jesus Christ like never before and learn how to break free from negative emotions and carnal mindsets to walk in the freedom, joy, and power of the Spirit of God. Reading this book will absolutely transform your walk with God and show you how to walk in the victory and love of Jesus Christ.

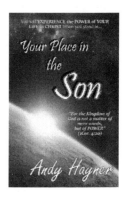

Jesus Christ died to give you the authority and power to heal the sick. **Born to Heal** will show you how to walk in the power and love of Jesus Christ and heal the sick as a lifestyle. Never again will you feel helpless in the face of sickness and pain. This book is packed with Biblical and practical training that will revolutionize your life!

Andy Hayner

The ***Born to Heal Interactive Training Manual*** is a powerful tool to learn the life-changing content of *Born to Heal* in small groups through direct interaction with the Scriptures. This is perfect to use even for those who have not read Born to Heal, or can be used for those who want to

supplement and reinforce what they read in Born to Heal. It's designed with LifeTeams, small groups, and discipleship relationships in mind. You'll **learn for yourself** *through interactive, inductive Bible studies and life-changing practical activation exercises.* The perfect resource for raising up supernatural disciples of Jesus Christ!

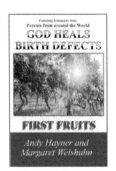

God Heals Birth Defects— First Fruits is a revolutionary book that will encourage, challenge, and equip you to minister healing in seemingly impossible situations. Written with a team of amazing parents from around the world, this book is packed with testimonies from parents who are seeing God heal their children who are afflicted with diagnosis such as autism, down syndrome, and cerebral palsy. If you are looking for hope and practical Biblical answers that will empower you to minister healing to those afflicted with birth defects, and are ready to step into a lifestyle that truly manifests "All things are possible with God," this book is for you!

Spirit Cry, is a powerful devotional tool that will accelerate your personal mind renewal and revolutionize your personal experience of God by adding incredible depth, insight, and power to your personal fellowship with God. You will learn how to use the Scriptures to speak to the Father as a Son and to hear the Father speak to you as a Son. Get this and unleash your Spirit Cry!

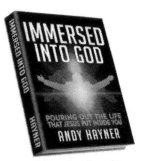

The book, *Immersed into God*, is comprehensive equipping to mobilize you to walk in the fullness of Jesus Christ and impact the world around you! Filled with examples, Biblical insights, and practical coaching, you will learn to experience God's power in your own life and to release His power to others by healing the sick, prophetic evangelism, and establishing disciples of Jesus Christ who walk in His supernatural power.

The *Immersed into God Interactive Training Manual* is a powerful tool to learn the life-changing content of *Immersed into God* in small groups, LifeTeams, and personal discipleship relationships. You'll **learn for yourself** *through interactive, inductive Bible studies and life-changing practical activation exercises.* This is the perfect resource for raising up supernatural disciples of Jesus Christ!

ABOUT THE AUTHOR

Andy Hayner is an experienced international conference speaker and dedicated disciple maker with a passion to mobilize believers to walk in the fullness of Jesus Christ worldwide. He is recognized for having a gift to impart a profound revelation of the believer's union with Jesus Christ in a simple, understandable way that unleashes greater depths of the love and power of God. Wherever Andy goes believers are equipped to heal the sick, reach the lost, and to walk in the fullness of Jesus. He has a passion for hands-on disciple making that has been developed through over twenty years of Christian service as a missionary, a pastor, a church planter, and Regional Director for John G. Lake Ministries, the oldest and most successful healing ministry in existence today. He is the founder of Full Speed Impact Ministries. He holds a Masters of Divinity from Columbia International University Graduate School of Missions. Andy remains a missionary at heart. He resides in Wisconsin with his wife and three children. You may direct ministry inquiries to FullSpeedAndy@gmail.com.

27406486R00043

Made in the USA
Columbia, SC
26 September 2018